First Ladies

Mamie
Eisenhower

Jill C. Wheeler

ABDO
Publishing Company

visit us at
www.abdopublishing.com

Published by ABDO Publishing Company, 8000 West 78th Street, Edina, Minnesota 55439.
Copyright © 2010 by Abdo Consulting Group, Inc. International copyrights reserved in all
countries. No part of this book may be reproduced in any form without written permission from the
publisher. The Checkerboard Library™ is a trademark and logo of ABDO Publishing Company.

Printed in the United States.

 Manufactured with paper containing at least 10% post-consumer waste

Cover Photo: Courtesy of the Dwight D. Eisenhower Presidential Library and Museum
Interior Photos: Alamy p. 27; Corbis pp. 19, 25, 26; Courtesy of the Dwight D. Eisenhower
    Presidential Library and Museum pp. 6, 7, 9, 10, 11, 12, 14, 15, 16, 17, 21;
    Getty Images pp. 5, 22

Series Coordinator: BreAnn Rumsch
Editors: Megan M. Gunderson, BreAnn Rumsch
Art Direction & Cover Design: Neil Klinepier

Library of Congress Cataloging-in-Publication Data

Wheeler, Jill C., 1964-
  Mamie Eisenhower / Jill C. Wheeler.
    p. cm. -- (First ladies)
  Includes index.
  ISBN 978-1-60453-630-0
  1. Eisenhower, Mamie Doud, 1896-1979--Juvenile literature. 2. Presidents' spouses--United
States--Biography--Juvenile literature. I. Title.

  E837.W47 2010
  973.921092--dc22
  [B]

                                2009009989

Contents

Mamie Eisenhower

Mamie Eisenhower was the first woman to become First Lady after **World War II** ended. Her husband was Dwight D. "Ike" Eisenhower, the thirty-fourth president of the United States.

Before she was First Lady, Mrs. Eisenhower spent many years as an army wife. She endured difficult living conditions and years of separation from her husband. Yet through these challenges, the Eisenhowers had a good marriage. They also maintained a strong tradition of service to their country.

World War II was a difficult time in the United States. The war touched nearly every American family. Millions of U.S. military members were involved in the war. In fact, Mrs. Eisenhower's husband led many of them as a general.

During the war, Mrs. Eisenhower was admired for her traditional values. While First Lady, Americans continued to appreciate her focus on home and family. Mrs. Eisenhower was not afraid to be herself. With her outgoing and genuine personality, she became one of the nation's most popular First Ladies.

Mamie Eisenhower was a likable First Lady. She was also a steady support for her husband while he served his country.

Victorian Childhood

Mamie Geneva Doud was born on November 14, 1896, in Boone, Iowa. She was the second of four girls. Her sisters were Eleanor, Ida Mae, and Mabel.

Mamie's parents were Elvira Carlson and John Sheldon Doud. Elvira's parents had moved to the United States from Sweden in the 1860s. John was from a wealthy family in Chicago, Illinois. He had moved to Boone for work in 1893 and soon met Elvira. They were married in 1894.

The Doud family's Denver home

The Doud family moved to Cedar Rapids, Iowa, less than one year after Mamie was born. When she was seven, they moved to Colorado. The family lived in

Colorado Springs for a short time before settling in Denver. There, the Douds moved to a wealthy neighborhood.

Mamie's parents lived by **Victorian** principles. They cared deeply about outward appearances. Mamie's father was **strict** with his children. Still, they often had fun. Mamie and her sisters played cards and rode bicycles and horses. And each summer, they spent time with their grandparents in Boone.

Mamie (far right) *with her family*

A Proper Education

In the early 1900s, Denver became a popular summertime vacation spot. Many wealthy people traveled there. They enjoyed attending fancy parties, dinners, and other social events.

The Douds were not luxuriant entertainers. Yet, they often hosted open houses on Sunday evenings. Friends would drop by for conversation and informal dinners. The Douds also spent much time together as a family. They enjoyed camping, fishing, and attending picnics and band concerts.

Young Mamie was like many other girls of her time. She was expected to grow up to take care of a home and a family. However, she was also expected to get a formal education.

Mamie attended elementary school at Corona Street School. Later, she attended East Denver High School. When Mamie was 14, the Douds began spending their winters in Texas. They rented a comfortable home in San Antonio. When there, Mamie attended Mulholland School.

Mamie was an independent girl. While she was growing up, women began to seek more independence. They wanted the freedom to make their own decisions. Mamie wanted this right, too.

Mamie did well in school. Still, her parents felt it was more important that she pass her classes than get top grades. They believed Mamie also needed to learn how to behave in society and run a household. So she studied sewing, piano, and ballroom dancing outside of school.

I Like Ike

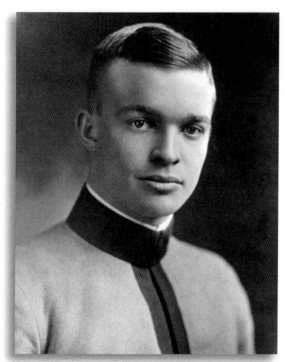

Ike graduated from the U.S. Military Academy at West Point in 1915.

At the time, prominent families sent their daughters to finishing school. This helped prepare them for social activities and marriage. So in 1914, Mamie began attending Miss Wolcott's in Denver.

Mamie quickly became one of Denver's most enchanting young women. She had many suitors who took her to movies, dinners, picnics, and dances.

Then in fall 1915, Mamie decided to leave Miss Wolcott's. She wanted to go to Texas with her family. In San Antonio, Mamie soon met someone who would change her life. That October, she went to Fort Sam

Houston to visit a family friend. There, several young officers introduced her to Dwight D. "Ike" Eisenhower. Mamie learned Ike was a lieutenant in the U.S. Army. He was from Abilene, Kansas.

Ike invited Mamie on a walk. The two liked each other right away and soon began dating. Ike took Mamie to restaurants, dances, and **vaudeville** shows. They enjoyed their time together, and their friendship soon turned into something special. On February 14, 1916, Ike and Mamie became engaged.

For their engagement, Ike gave Mamie a copy of his West Point class ring.

Military Wife

At first, Mamie's parents were concerned. They thought she and Ike were rushing into marriage. They also knew military life would be very challenging. Yet Mamie was not going to change her mind.

Mamie and Ike agreed to marry once she turned 20 years old. However, their plans soon changed. Ike worried he might be

stationed somewhere new. So on July 1, 1916, the couple married. The ceremony took place at the Doud home in Denver. Mamie was 19 years old, and Ike was 25.

Now, Mamie had to adjust to being a military wife. Her mother and father's warnings had been right. This new life would be much different from her comfortable childhood. Mamie had to manage all the household chores herself. Yet, she had never cooked or even made her own bed before!

While Ike served in the army, the couple lived at various military bases. Military housing was functional, but it offered few luxuries. In fact, one of their early homes was heated by a wood stove. Another had no kitchen. Mamie had to wash dishes and do laundry in the bathtub!

In addition, Ike's army salary did not go far. Yet as a girl, Mamie's father had taught her the value of money. From early on, she skillfully managed their small budget.

Over the years, military life presented Mamie with many challenges. Yet, she and Ike maintained a loving marriage.

Trials and Travels

Mrs. Eisenhower's life was very different from the lives of her friends in Denver. As she quickly discovered, military life was one of service and sacrifice. It tested her strength. Yet, her love for her husband helped her adjust without giving up. She was determined to be a partner in Mr. Eisenhower's career.

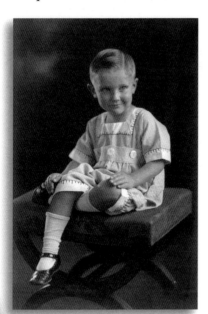

Every year after Icky's death, Mr. Eisenhower sent his wife yellow roses on September 24.

In April 1917, the United States entered **World War I**. Mr. Eisenhower now had much work to do with the military. He was often away on military assignments. At home, Mrs. Eisenhower learned to get by on her own.

Without her husband, Mrs. Eisenhower welcomed their first son on September 24, 1917. She named the baby Doud Dwight. He was nicknamed Little Ike but soon called Icky.

During their time in Panama, the Eisenhowers lived at Camp Gaillard.

For the next two years, Mrs. Eisenhower raised Icky mostly by herself. At the end of 1920, tragedy struck. Icky became sick with **scarlet fever** just before Christmas. He died on January 2, 1921. The death was a heartbreaking setback for the Eisenhowers.

In early 1922, the army sent Mr. Eisenhower to the **Panama Canal Zone**. Mrs. Eisenhower did not enjoy the tropical weather there. So, she only lived in Panama off and on. Their son John Sheldon Doud was born in Denver on August 3, 1922.

In 1928, the Eisenhower family moved to Paris, France. Mrs. Eisenhower enjoyed life in Paris. She managed the household and took French lessons. Mr. and Mrs. Eisenhower attended parties, hosted dinners, and went dancing. As a family, they toured the city. They also traveled to Italy and Germany. In 1929, they returned to America.

Mr. Eisenhower was transferred to the Philippines in 1935. Mrs. Eisenhower did not look forward to the tropical weather there. But, she knew her husband needed her support. So in October 1936, she joined him in the Philippines. There, Mrs. Eisenhower worked to help her husband's career. She also kept busy with various social activities. Mrs. Eisenhower tried to enjoy life in the Philippines, but she missed home.

Then in spring 1939, the Eisenhowers were ordered back to the United States. They relocated to Fort Lewis near Tacoma, Washington. There, Mrs. Eisenhower kept house and often fed her husband's unexpected lunchtime guests. She helped redecorate the Officers' Club and was active in the Women's Club. And, she volunteered at the American Red Cross.

In 1941, the Eisenhowers received good news. Mr. Eisenhower was ordered back to Fort Sam Houston. The Eisenhowers were happy to return to San Antonio. Not long after, Mr. Eisenhower was promoted to general.

Mrs. Eisenhower brought John with her to the Philippines. John later followed in his father's footsteps by joining the military.

World War II

On December 7, 1941, Mrs. Eisenhower was listening to the radio. She heard news of the Japanese attack on the U.S. naval base at Pearl Harbor, Hawaii. The next day, the United States entered **World War II**.

In June, 1942, Mr. Eisenhower was sent to England to help fight the war. While he was gone, Mrs. Eisenhower lived in Washington, D.C. She didn't see her husband for nearly three years.

Communication during the war was limited. For security reasons, no phone calls were allowed. So, the Eisenhowers depended on letters to keep their marriage strong. They exchanged several hundred over the course of the war.

In the meantime, Mrs. Eisenhower volunteered with the Red Cross. She also helped at a canteen where soldiers came to eat. On May 8, 1945, the war ended in Europe. Mr. Eisenhower returned home in June.

During the war, Mr. Eisenhower's role and visibility had greatly increased. By the time the war ended, he had become a five-star general. This success had also turned Mrs. Eisenhower into a public figure. She knew it was important to set a good example for Americans. So, she always acted with courage.

Mrs. Eisenhower continued to support the Red Cross as First Lady.

To the White House

After **World War II**, Mrs. Eisenhower looked forward to finally settling down. In October 1948, Mr. Eisenhower retired from active military duty. He then became president of Columbia University. So, the Eisenhowers moved to New York City, New York. Yet, their quiet life there did not last long.

President Harry S. Truman called Mr. Eisenhower back into service in 1950. President Truman appointed him the first Supreme Allied Commander of **NATO**. So in 1951, Mr. Eisenhower went to Europe.

For the second time, Mrs. Eisenhower moved to Paris with her husband. There, she often entertained important officials. She also became friends with several European leaders.

Back in the United States, Mr. Eisenhower was a war hero. In June 1952, he agreed to run for president as a **Republican**. Mrs. Eisenhower had once again been looking forward to quieter years. Yet, she supported her husband's decision. She recognized this was a chance for him to serve his country.

Mr. Eisenhower's campaign used the **slogan** "I Like Ike." Meanwhile, Mrs. Eisenhower's popularity grew. Many people even said, "I like Ike, but I LOVE Mamie." She attracted many women voters. In November, Mr. Eisenhower won the election in a landslide!

During the campaign, the Eisenhowers went on a whistle-stop tour. They were laid back and friendly. One morning, they even wore their bathrobes to greet a crowd of spectators!

First Lady Next Door

On January 20, 1953, Mr. Eisenhower became the nation's thirty-fourth president. Mrs. Eisenhower was now the First Lady. Americans easily connected with her. They liked that her life revolved around her family and her home.

With her warm smile, Mrs. Eisenhower made people feel comfortable. She happily greeted White House tour groups. During her husband's first term, she shook hands with more than 100,000 people! She also replied to thousands of the letters Americans wrote to her.

Mrs. Eisenhower's popularity influenced American style. She loved the color pink, and she often used it in clothing and decorating. Soon, "First Lady Pink" became the most popular color of the 1950s.

Over the years, Mrs. Eisenhower hosted events for 37 world leaders. This was more than any previous First Lady! In addition, she threw her support behind numerous organizations. These included Girl Scouts of the USA, the New York Association for the Blind, and the American Heart Association.

The First Lady strongly supported **civil rights**, too. She believed in giving African Americans equal opportunities. So, she invited African-American singer Marian Anderson to perform at the U.S. Capitol. Mrs. Eisenhower was also the first First Lady to invite African-American children to the annual Easter Egg Roll.

Mrs. Eisenhower loved hosting people at the White House. She devoted much effort to making her guests feel welcome.

The President's Wife

The First Lady felt her most important job was to support the president. She worked hard to make the White House feel like home. Mrs. Eisenhower managed the White House staff like a five-star general! She also oversaw the family's budget. She always took steps to save money, such as clipping grocery coupons. The Eisenhowers even ate their leftovers.

Mrs. Eisenhower also made sure her husband took time to relax. She believed in separating his work life

Beauty on a Budget

As an army wife, Mrs. Eisenhower left her stamp on numerous military quarters. She always found ways to make inexpensive improvements to each home. As First Lady, she used this experience to personalize the White House on a tight budget.

Through small projects, Mrs. Eisenhower hoped to help preserve White House history. First, she located several pieces of historic furniture. She had them displayed in the White House. She also worked to find china pieces that represented each president. The china collection was completed in 1959. It is still displayed in the White House China Room today.

The White House china collection includes both official state china sets and several personal sets.

from his home life. The Eisenhowers enjoyed quiet evenings together in their private rooms at the White House. There, they often ate dinner on trays in front of the television.

Even with Mrs. Eisenhower's efforts, the president had serious health problems by 1955. That fall, he had a heart attack. In spring 1956, doctors operated on his intestine. Mrs. Eisenhower stayed by his side during his recovery. When he returned to work, she carefully monitored his schedule.

President Eisenhower still felt a strong sense of duty to his country. So, Mrs. Eisenhower encouraged him to run for a second term. In fall 1956, President Eisenhower won reelection. He began his next term in January 1957.

Home at Last

The Eisenhowers stayed busy for the next four years. But in 1961, they were ready to retire. They moved to a farm near Gettysburg, Pennsylvania. They had purchased the home in 1950, but had not yet lived there.

For the next eight years, the Eisenhowers lived a quiet life. They entertained friends and family, including four grandchildren. They also helped complete the Dwight D. Eisenhower Presidential Library and Museum in Abilene, Kansas. It opened in 1966.

In 1965 and 1968, Mr. Eisenhower's health continued to suffer. He had two heart attacks.

Mrs. Eisenhower became the first First Lady to receive protection as a widow from the Secret Service.

The Eisenhowers are buried in the Place of Meditation. This building is located at the Dwight D. Eisenhower Presidential Library and Museum. Their son Icky is also buried there.

He later died on March 28, 1969. Ten years later, Mrs. Eisenhower suffered a **stroke**. She died on November 1, 1979. She was buried next to her husband at the Eisenhower Library.

Mamie Eisenhower was a popular First Lady. After **World War II**, Americans wanted stability. Mrs. Eisenhower represented the traditional values needed at that time. She had a strong sense of duty to her country and her family.

Timeline

1896	On November 14, Mamie Geneva Doud was born.
1915	Mamie finished her formal education at Miss Wolcott's finishing school.
1916	On July 1, Mamie married Dwight D. "Ike" Eisenhower.
1917	The Eisenhowers' son Doud Dwight was born on September 24.
1921	On January 2, Doud died from scarlet fever.
1922	The Eisenhowers' son John Sheldon Doud was born on August 3.
1941	On December 8, the United States entered World War II.
1945	In May, World War II ended in Europe; Mr. Eisenhower returned home in June.
1953–1961	Mrs. Eisenhower acted as First Lady, while her husband served as president.
1966	The Dwight D. Eisenhower Presidential Library and Museum opened.
1969	Mr. Eisenhower died on March 28.
1979	On November 1, Mrs. Eisenhower died.

Mamie Eisenhower stood 5 feet 1 inch (1.5 m) tall. She had reddish brown hair and blue eyes.

Mrs. Eisenhower's favorite flower was the pink sweetheart rose.

Mrs. Eisenhower enjoyed playing cards. She especially liked the games bridge and canasta.

Tourists can visit the Mamie Doud Eisenhower Birthplace Museum in Boone, Iowa.

In 1952, Mrs. Eisenhower was honored in France with the Cross of Merit. She earned this award for unselfish service to mankind.

Mrs. Eisenhower is the first First Lady to be featured in television campaigning.

The first songs written for a presidential candidate's wife were written for Mrs. Eisenhower in 1952. They are "Mamie" and "I Want Mamie."

A 1969 Gallup public opinion poll named Mrs. Eisenhower the most admired woman in the world.

Glossary

civil rights - the individual rights of a citizen, such as the right to vote or freedom of speech.

NATO - North Atlantic Treaty Organization. A group formed by the United States, Canada, and some European countries in 1949. It tries to create peace among its nations and protect them from common enemies.

Panama Canal - a human-made, narrow canal across Panama that connects the Atlantic and Pacific oceans. The Canal Zone was an area that began in the center of the canal and extended five miles (8 km) on each side.

Republican - a member of the Republican political party. Republicans are conservative and believe in small government.

scarlet fever - a disease marked by a red rash and swelling of the nose, the throat, and the mouth.

slogan - a word or a phrase used to express a position, a stand, or a goal.

strict - demanding others to follow rules or regulations in a rigid, exact manner.

stroke - a sudden loss of consciousness, sensation, and voluntary motion. This attack of paralysis is caused by a rupture to a blood vessel of the brain, often caused by a blood clot.

vaudeville (VAWD-vuhl) - stage entertainment consisting of several acts such as dancers, singers, comedians, and acrobats.

Victorian - relating to moral standards, attitudes, and conduct during the reign of Queen Victoria of England in the 1800s.

World War I - from 1914 to 1918, fought in Europe. Great Britain, France, Russia, the United States, and their allies were on one side. Germany, Austria-Hungary, and their allies were on the other side.

World War II - from 1939 to 1945, fought in Europe, Asia, and Africa. Great Britain, France, the United States, the Soviet Union, and their allies were on one side. Germany, Italy, Japan, and their allies were on the other side.

Web Sites

To learn more about Mamie Eisenhower, visit ABDO Publishing Company on the World Wide Web at **www.abdopublishing.com**. Web sites about Mamie Eisenhower are featured on our Book Links page. These links are routinely monitored and updated to provide the most current information available.

Index